NASCAR

Written by Paul Stevenson

CONTENTS

All words in **BOLD** can be found in the glossary.

First published in 2024 by
Hungry Tomato Ltd
F15, Old Bakery Studios,
Blewetts Wharf, Malpas Road,
Truro, Cornwall,
TR1 1QH, UK.

A CIP catalog record for this book is available from the
British Library.

ISBN 9781915461896
Manufactured in the USA

Discover more at
www.hungrytomato.com

This is...
NASCAR!

SPEED!

NASCAR is where speed rules and being fast is number one. Drivers live for it and fans get hooked on it!

STARS!

2016 - Jimmie Johnson made a record-tying seventh NASCAR premier series title, joining the NASCAR Hall of Fame and making history!

Jimmie Johnson

SPILLS!

2022 - A rainstorm caused a huge pile-up at Daytona. The crash wiped out 20 cars!

WHAT DOES NASCAR STAND FOR?

National Association
of Stock Car Auto Racing

CIRCUITS AND RACES

THEN...

The first NASCAR races started in 1948 at Daytona, Florida, USA. Daytona was a 1.5-mile beach and road circuit.

Souped-up saloon cars, such as Oldsmobiles, were soon the standard NASCAR racer.

1950 - NASCAR driver Red Byron races on Daytona Beach in a souped-up Oldsmobile

NOW...

Daytona is the biggest event in NASCAR. It's the Daytona 500 that kicks off the season.

Race crew trailers, equipment and camper vans

Track length is just under 2.5 miles

The grandstand marks the start and finish of the race

Tailgating area for fans

NASCAR has 4 main national racing series:

- The NASCAR Cup Series
- The Xfinity Series
- The Craftsman Truck Series
- The ARCA Menards Series

There are 4 main types of track: short tracks, intermediate ovals, super speedways and road circuits.

A crash on the banked track of the North Carolina Speedway, USA

Speedways are all **banked**, left-hand turn race tracks. They have a concrete or tarmac surface.

Road circuits are normal roads that have been closed for a race. They are a tough test of a driver's skills. On road circuits, drivers have to make left-hand and right-hand turns.

Martinsville is a speedway circuit. It is the shortest of all the circuits at just over half a mile long.

Martinsville Speedway, Virginia, USA

Road America in Wisconsin is the longest NASCAR track. It is just over 4 miles long.

NASCAR TRACKS

NASCAR hold races at 42 venues in the US and Canada. The track types include:

Short speedways: Under 1 mile
Speedways: 1 to 2.5 miles
Super Speedways: Over 2.5 miles
Road Circuits: Over 1.9 miles

NASCAR CUP RACE

In the regular cup race, stages of up to 40 cars line up on the starting line.

REGULAR SEASON...

In the NASCAR Cup Series, whether it's during the 26-race regular season or in the 10-race playoffs, there's no question that every point counts. Drivers win points for race wins, position finishes, and stage positions.

PLAYOFFS...

Playoff spots are given to the 16 drivers who win the most regular season races. If there aren't enough winners, those with the most points will progress to the playoffs.

THE TOP 12...

Now it gets harder! After the first playoff stages, only 12 qualify. After the second, 8 drivers qualify. After the third, it drops to the final 4 drivers, who then race to see who will be crowned the championship winner.

Celebrating after winning a NASCAR race

Jimmie Johnson wins the Ford EcoBoost 400 and the 2016 NASCAR Sprint Cup Championship

THE RACE - PIT CREW

Pit crews work long hours. They work away from home and are always on the move.

Crew members make sure the car is ready to pass inspection by race officials. The car set-up must pass race rules and regulations.

If the car doesn't pass the pre-race inspection, it isn't going to make the starting grid!

The rules say what size a car can be. They also say how low to the ground it can be, and what type of fuel can be used. After the race, officials check again to make sure no rules have been broken.

The cars are taken back home to base on trucks.

The race car engines have to be rebuilt for the next race!

IN THE HOT SEAT

There is a real buzz at the start of each and every race.

It's hot in the driver's seat, but drivers have to wear **Nomex** flame-retardant suits, in case of fire.

A **pace car** leads the 40 cars on warm-up laps before the race. These increase in speed, allowing a flying start to the race.

In just a few seconds, cars can average 200 mph!

The starts are a bit scary, and some cars don't even finish the first lap!

CRASH!

There are very few NASCAR races
where there hasn't been a crash!

Crashes can be spectacular
because of the high speeds

"You win some, lose some and wreck some" - Dale Earnhardt, legendary NASCAR driver

TACTICS

Drafting a car like this breaks the force of air, making you **aerodynamic.**

It gives the **trailing** driver a **slingshot** effect when trying to pull out and pass a car ahead of them. This can make a huge difference to the race results, as the driver waits until the final laps to steal the lead!

Getting close has its dangers. You can get a nudge! Then you will be aero loose or aero tight.

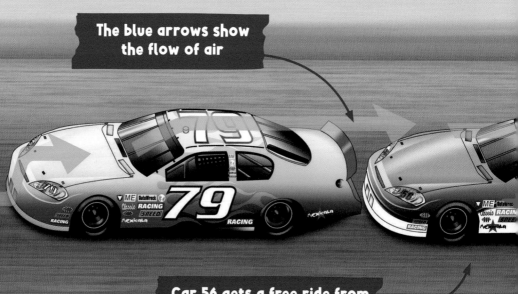

The blue arrows show the flow of air

Car 56 gets a free ride from car 79, thanks to drafting

Aero loose is when the back end of the car starts spinning and sliding in a different direction.

Aero tight is when the car won't turn. Worn tires can cause this to happen, too.

There's no time for drivers to react because they are going so fast.

Aero loose

You're just gone!

PITTING

Yellow flags are waved by officials to alert drivers to crashes or hazards ahead. Drivers will then have to follow the pace car until the track is cleared.

Pace car

It's sometimes a good time to take a pit stop. Winning a race isn't all about speed; having a good strategy in place for pit stops can be the key to success.

The pit crew must work very quickly, as they can be the difference between the driver winning or losing a race!

With the NASCAR Next Gen car, four-tire pit stops have come down to 8.6 seconds. Every second counts!

Depending on the type of track, you may see 2-6 pit stops in a race.

Each pit crew is given certain jobs, managed by the crew chief, who tells them what to do and how.

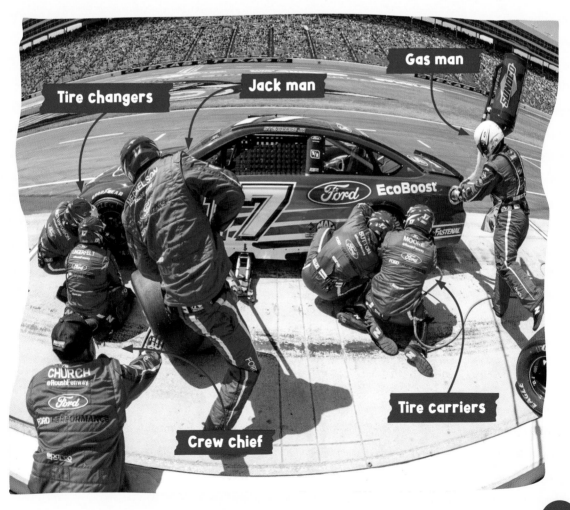

Gas man

Jack man

Tire changers

Tire carriers

Crew chief

DRIVERS HALL OF FAME

RICHARD PETTY

- Competed in over 1,000 races
- 200 race wins
- 7 championship wins
- Retired in 1992

"No one wants to quit when they're losing and no one wants to quit when they're winning." - **Richard Petty**

"Petty broke too many bones to count. He drove with cracked ribs, and even a broken neck. He was racing cool – the fans' favorite." - **Tom Jensen, sports writer**

DALE EARNHARDT, AKA THE INTIMIDATOR

- Competed in 676 races
- 76 race wins
- 7 championship wins
- Died, aged 49, in the 2001 Daytona 500.

"You've got to be closer to the edge than ever to win. That means sometimes you go over the edge."
Dale Earnhardt

DID YOU KNOW?

Dale Earnhardt Junior won at Daytona just 5 months after his father died there.

JIMMIE JOHNSON

- Competed in over 650 races
- 83 race wins
- 7 championship wins
- Started competing at 5 years old and at 8 won his first motor racing championship.

"Since I was a kid, what's drawn me to racing is the feeling inside of me, the passion I have for the sport, the feeling I have while competing and doing what I do in a car..." - **Jimmie Johnson**

COOL NASCAR FACTS

1. The first NASCAR race took place on a beach!

2. NASCAR cars generate enough downforce to drive upside down.

3. Drivers experience up to **3Gs** of force on their necks.

4. The most wrecks in a single race (in modern NASCAR history) was in 2002 at Talladega on lap 14; 31 cars were involved!

5. The first Daytona 500 took place in February 1959. Lee Petty was anounced the winner, by a photo finish. The race was so close that it took over 2 days to announce!

Joey Logano wins the Ambetter Health 400 Race in 2023 NASCAR Cup Series

THE XFINITY SERIES

The Xfinity series is a stock car racing series, run by NASCAR.

It is NASCAR's second-tier circuit to the Cup Series, top level.

The Xfinity Series was formed in the 1950s as a short track race division. The modern-day Xfinity Series was formed in 1982.

NASCAR Xfinity Series events are often held as a **support race**, the day before a Cup Series event.

TRUCK RACING

The truck races are for modified pick-up trucks. The races are run over 200-250 miles.

The NASCAR SuperTruck Series was launched in 1995. Today, it's called the NASCAR Craftsman Truck Series.

Truck drivers play rough, too!

NASCAR IS THE LOUDEST, ROUGHEST, TOUGHEST MOTORSPORT IN THE WORLD!

Top speeds of up to 180 mph!

BE A DRIVER

How do I become a NASCAR race car driver?

- Most drivers start young. Some start as early as 4 years old! They begin by racing karts or midget racing cars at their local racetrack.

- Talent will soon have you moving up from amateur local races to events **sponsored** by big-name companies.

- Keep trying and you may catch the attention of one of the big teams scouting for new drivers.

- You need a desire to succeed and the energy and ambition to work hard. Being a good mechanic will help, too.

AND, FINALLY, YOU MUST KEEP FIT!

GLOSSARY

3G - a pull three times the force of gravity.

aerodynamic - a shape that helps a car cut through air so that it goes faster.

banked - a track that is sloped.

drafting - (see also: **trailing**) a technique where a car follows close behind one car, reducing overall drag. They travel faster together than seperately.

modified - a car that has been changed and made more powerful.

Nomex - a fire-resistant material used to make race suits.

pace car - a fast, powerful car that leads a parade of race cars when they need to remain below racing speed.

slingshot - something that gives a catapult effect.

sponsor - a company that pays for the car and mechanics, usually in exchange for advertisement of their company. Many cars have their sponsor's logo on them.

support race - a lower-ranked racing event for fans to watch before the main event.

tailgating - partying and camping in the back of a car or truck during a sporting event.

trailing - (see also: **drafting**) following closely behind another car.

venue - the place where an event is being held.

yellow flag - the flag shown after a crash or if there is debris on the track. Overtaking is not allowed at this time.

INDEX

Picture credits:
(t=top; b=bottom; c=center; l=left; r=right):
Shutterstock: Action sports 14b; EPG_EuroPhotoGraphics 20m; Grindstone Media Group 1, 4, 5tr, 11, 14-15t; 21b, 22b, 23br, 25, 26-27, 30cr; HodagMedia 29. Action Plus: 8c. Chris Graythen/ Getty Images: 5c. Chris McGrath/ Getty Images: 12, 13b. Chris O'Meara/ AP/ PA Photos: 23t. George Tiedemann/ GT Images/ Corbis: 9, 22t. James Powell: 18-19. Jeff Hayes/ AFP/ Getty Images: 24b. Jon Feingersh/ Getty Images: 15br. Jonathan Ferrey/ Getty Images for NASCAR: 13t. RacingOne/ Getty Images: 6b. Reuters/ Corbis: 28c. Reuters/ Pierre Ducharme: 19tr. Richard Francis/ Action Plus: 7. Sam Sharpe/ The Sharpe Image/ Corbis: 16-17. ticktock Media Archive: 6t.

Every effort has been made to trace the copyright holders, and we apologize in advance for any unintentional omissions. We would be pleased to insert the appropriate acknowledgments in any subsequent edition of this publication.